From
Rags to Riches

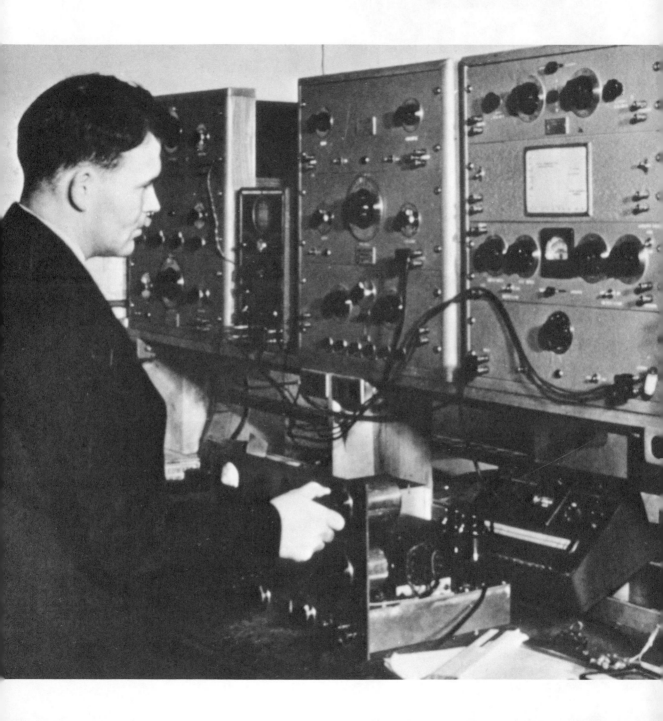

From Rags to Riches

People Who Started Businesses from Scratch

by Nathan Aaseng

 Lerner Publications Company
Minneapolis

To Michael

Page 1: William Procter and James Gamble started out making soap and candles in a rented storeroom. In the early 1850s, they moved their operation to a large manufacturing plant.

Page 2: Bill Hewlett tests one of Hewlett-Packard's early products, an audio oscillator.

Library of Congress Cataloging-in-Publication Data

Aaseng, Nathan.
  From rags to riches : people who started businesses from scratch /
by Nathan Aaseng.
      p.   cm.
  Includes bibliographical references.
  Summary: Presents brief biographies of the enterprising
individuals who started such products and companies as Apple
computers, Sears, the Dow Jones Index and The Wall Street Journal,
J.C. Penney, Hershey's chocolate, and Kinney shoes.
  ISBN 0-8225-0679-3 (lib. bdg.)
  1. Success in business—United States—Case studies—Juvenile
literature. [1. Businessmen. 2. Business enterprises.]
I. Title.
HF5386.A387   1990
650.1'092'273—dc20
[B]   89-13059
[920]   CIP
                                                               AC

Manufactured in the United States of America

1 2 3 4 5 6 7 8 9 10 99 98 97 96 95 94 93 92 91 90

Contents

Introduction

THE TRADITIONAL "AMERICAN DREAM" holds that, in the free-enterprise system of the United States, any person, no matter how poor, can achieve great things. The business world is full of inspiring stories of people from humble origins who were able to achieve that dream.

Where did the Apple computer, HERSHEY'S milk chocolate bars, or Tide detergent come from? How did giant corporations such as Sears, Marriott, and J.C. Penney come into our lives?

The size, wealth, and influence of these businesses and the success of their products often gives the mistaken impression that they are the work of a group of incredibly wealthy people. The image that people hold of "big business" is that of a group of faceless money magicians performing mysterious

Left: George Kinney stands in front of his first shoe store in Waverly, New York. The man in the apron is Milner Kemp, Kinney's first employee.

financial dealings which most of us could never begin to understand.

In reality, though, even the largest corporations and the most famous products started with one or two people. The products you find around your house or the services you find in town are there because some person came up with an idea and was able to turn it into something saleable. Certainly money is an important factor in guaranteeing the success of a business. But it has not always been necessary. Most of the famous products and companies were started by ordinary people like you and me—many of them by people who were far poorer than you or I will ever be.

Sam Walton, founder of the Wal-Mart chain of stores, was a teenager during the Great Depression. His father, a banker, struggled to feed the family during the worst of the depression. Sam Walton delivered newspapers, milked cows, and delivered milk to earn extra money for the family. He became one of the wealthiest people in the United States.

A Chinese engineering student named An Wang immigrated to the United States during World War II, and began his own company. The company was making only $10,000 a year when Wang licensed one of his inventions to IBM for $400,000. Within 30 years, Wang Laboratories was the largest supplier of word processors in the world.

The person behind Kinney Shoe Company had to overcome not only poverty but great tragedy as

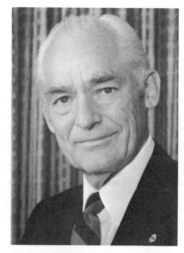

Sam Walton

An Wang

well. George Kinney grew up destitute after his parents' general store failed. Life grew even harsher for him at the age of nine, when his father died. Years later, Kinney worked his way from stock clerk to manager of a Waverly, New York, shoe store. Just when he thought the bad times were past, his wife of two years died in childbirth, and Kinney was left to raise his son alone. He managed gamely until his employer went bankrupt, which put Kinney out of a job.

In desperation, Kinney pulled together his small savings and bought as many of the shoes as he could. He then thought of selling shoes for the whole family instead of specializing in men's and women's shoes. He also sold his shoes at discount prices. The idea proved so popular that he was able to start a second store within the year. From there business kept snowballing until Kinney Shoe stores were located throughout the country.

The stories that follow tell similar tales in more detail. Read on and learn the stories of the people behind such familiar businesses as Apple, Sears, Dow Jones, J.C. Penney, Hewlett-Packard, and Hershey.

Small Size.
IVORY
REG. U. S. PAT. OFF.
SOAP
Procter & Gamble, Cincinnati

Living off the Fat of the Land

Procter & Gamble

The pork **industry** refers to the group of farmers, stockyard operators, and meat packers who are involved in making pork available to consumers. The word *industry* can also be used more generally to mean all of a nation's manufacturing activity.

A **waste product** is what is left over after the main product has been used or taken out.

IN THE 1830S, THE RIVER TOWN OF CINcinnati, Ohio, was thriving, thanks in part to the growth of its pork industry. The processing of pork naturally meant that there was an abundance of animal fat in the city. While grease and fat are considered to be waste products, they can be used to make at least two products: soap and candles.

By making soap and candles, two poor immigrants built a business that would dominate the household products market in the United States. There is scarcely a person in the country who has not bought some of the products made by the firm that William Procter and James Gamble founded. Their names have been linked for more than 150 years, guaranteeing them a place in history as one of the most famous duos that ever lived.

James Gamble

William Procter

Both Procter and Gamble fled to the United States to seek a better life for themselves. The Gamble family, including 16-year-old James, arrived first, in 1819, from Ireland. They had intended to settle in Shawneetown, Illinois. James Gamble would have never met William Procter if he hadn't become seriously ill while the family was en route. The boat on which the Gambles were traveling docked at Cincinnati so James could be treated. While waiting for him to recover, the family took a liking to the city and stayed.

Two years later, James found work as a soap-maker's apprentice. Although soap making was an uncomplicated process, Gamble was obliged by trade standards to study under the master soap-maker for eight years. In 1829, free to go into business on his

In the 19th century, a young person often became an **apprentice** to a skilled worker to learn a skill or trade like soap making. The apprentice worked for little or no money but gained experience. Later, most people began attending colleges, universities, or vocational schools to learn a trade.

Elizabeth (Norris) Gamble

Olivia (Norris) Procter

Manufacturers need **raw materials** to make products. For Procter's candles and Gamble's soaps, one of the raw materials was animal fat.

own, he formed a partnership with a man named Hiram Knowlton.

In 1832 the London woolen-goods shop owned by 31-year-old William Procter was robbed. Having lost everything, Procter and his wife decided to make a fresh start and move to the United States. Sadly, the Procters' bad fortune followed them across the Atlantic Ocean. They arrived in the United States just as the country was going through a cholera epidemic. Before they could reach their destination, Mrs. Procter died of the disease.

Procter settled in Cincinnati. He had no clear idea of how he would make money to support himself. But he quickly discovered that high-quality candles were scarce in the city of 25,000, despite a wealth of raw materials for making them. He had worked in a candle shop as a boy, and Procter thought he knew enough about candle making to go into business.

Procter and Gamble met when Procter married the sister of Gamble's wife in 1833. Their father-in-law pointed out that, since the two used the same raw materials for their products, they might consider pooling their efforts. Eventually Procter and Gamble agreed. In 1837 Gamble pulled out of Knowlton & Gamble and combined his business with Procter's.

Procter's facilities consisted of a rented storeroom, a yard, and a doghouse. The doghouse was Procter's way of discouraging burglars. Too poor to keep a watchdog, Procter had simply attached a chain to the doghouse and had flung bones around the yard so it would appear as though there was a dog.

Gamble and Procter boiled the fat for their products outside in a huge wooden kettle that was fitted with an iron bottom. Gamble took responsibility for keeping the pot full. Each morning he knocked on the doors of houses and hotels, offering bars of soap in exchange for fat and meat scraps.

It soon became evident that Procter was better skilled for selling and finance, while Gamble was better at running the factory. The two trusted each other enough to let each handle his area of expertise without interference. In fact, despite their friendship, they were so preoccupied with their own ends of the business that they rarely spoke to each other during their business hours.

At first the company made most of its money on candles, but soap gradually became the more popular product. Success was not immediate. In fact, the company was still operating out of its rented storeroom in 1850.

One of the reasons Procter & Gamble began to prosper was its reputation for honesty in a time when cheating was commonplace. Unlike many competitors, Procter & Gamble did not rig its scales to report false weights, nor did it substitute such things as marble dust, flour, and glue for the more expensive soap ingredients. The company ran into problems, however, because many stores cut the soap they sold from a large slab without any manufacturer

Procter & Gamble's trademark started with this crude cross that was used by dockhands to distinguish boxes that held the company's candles from other boxes loaded aboard ships.

In time the identifying mark used by dockhands was switched to a star within a circle.

The first trademark actually used by Procter & Gamble itself was a roughly drawn moon and stars.

The 1882 version of moon and stars was registered with the U.S. Patent and Trademark Office.

Further embellishments had been added to the trademark by 1902.

Procter & Gamble simplified the trademark's design around 1920.

A **trademark** is a distinctive, legally protected symbol, title, or design used by a company to distinguish its products from those of other companies.

labels. Customers frequently had no way of knowing who made the soap they bought. The only result of Procter & Gamble's honesty, then, was to make its own operating costs higher than that of the less scrupulous competitors.

In 1851 a dockhand began marking packages of Procter & Gamble's Star brand candles with a cross. Eventually, this became a star, then a cluster of stars, and finally a moon and stars that became the Procter & Gamble trademark. These early markings served as identification to customers, telling them that it was a Procter & Gamble product, and not a cheap imitation. Sales increased quickly until, by 1859, Procter & Gamble was the one of the largest companies in Cincinnati.

Some shrewd strategy in 1860 further strengthened the company's position. Procter & Gamble predicted that the growing hostility between the North and South would threaten its supply of rosin. At the time, rosin was an important ingredient in soap, and it could only be bought from suppliers in the South. Procter & Gamble bought an enormous amount and stored it in a factory. When the Civil War began later that year, the price of rosin increased by 1,500 percent. Most Northern soap manufacturers were crippled by the high cost, but Procter & Gamble had plenty of rosin on hand to produce soap for a long time.

Because there was a scarcity of materials such as rosin and lard over the next two decades, Procter &

Harley Procter

James N. Gamble

Gamble searched for substitute ingredients. The company developed methods of making soap without lard and discovered a good substitute for rosin.

The company's most important new product in its early days was Ivory soap, which was developed by the second generation of Procters and Gambles. In the late 1870s, James N. Gamble, son of the co-founder, began looking for an economical way to produce a soap that would be the same quality as the most expensive soaps made (known as "castile" soaps). After four years of research, he perfected a formula using two kinds of fat and eight other ingredients.

At first the company simply called it "White Soap." Then William Procter's son, Harley, came up with a better name. While sitting in church one Sunday,

Procter & Gamble experimented to find different and better ways to make products. In a process called **research and development**, many companies conduct experiments to create new products or improve existing products. **Research** is investigation aimed at discovering new scientific knowledge. **Development** is the attempt to use new knowledge to make useful products or processes.

In 1930 the company had a sculptor design the logo that would be used, unchanged, for the next 50 years and beyond.

Advertising is the presentation of ideas, goods, and services to the public; it is paid for by a sponsor. Slogans, or themes, are intended to help the advertising audience remember the product and the message.

Manufacturers will often adopt **brand names** to help customers tell the difference between their products and other manufacturers' products. In addition to Ivory, some Procter & Gamble brand names are Crest, Tide, and Crisco.

he half listened to a reading of the 45th Psalm. The words "ivory palaces" triggered an instant reaction, and he decided right then to call the soap Ivory.

In order to prove that this less expensive soap was the equal of any soap on the market, Procter sent three samples of castile soap to a scientific laboratory, along with a bar of Ivory. The scientists reported that Ivory had fewer impurities than the others. According to the lab's analysis, Ivory was 99.44 percent free of impurities. Procter immediately latched on to the scientific-sounding "99 and 44/100 percent pure" as an advertising slogan. The slogan boosted sales considerably.

Another slogan—"It floats"—also helped Procter & Gamble to develop product identification for Ivory. Legend has it that the unusual floating feature happened accidentally. A worker is said to have left his mixing machine running during his lunch break. The extra-long mixing time forced air into the mixture, which caused the hardened soap to float. During an era in which many people took baths in rivers, this unusual floating soap was useful.

The new generation of Procter & Gamble executives, the founders' sons, recognized the value of advertising. The company began to spend a large amount of money promoting its products in newspapers and magazines and, later, on radio and television. As a result, Procter & Gamble established recognizable brand names early in its history. The company developed into the manufacturer of a vast

THE "IVORY" is a Laundry Soap, with all the fine qualities of a choice Toilet Soap, and is 99 44-100 **per cent. pure.**

Ladies will find this Soap especially adapted for washing laces, infants' clothing, silk hose, cleaning gloves and all articles of fine texture and delicate color, and for the varied uses about the house that daily arise, requiring the use of soap that is above the ordinary in quality.

For the Bath, Toilet, or Nursery it is preferred to most of the Soaps sold for toilet use, being purer and much more pleasant and effective and possessing all the desirable properties of the finest unadultered White Castile Soap. The Ivory Soap will **"float."**

The cakes are so shaped that they may be used entire for general purposes or divided with a stout thread (as illustrated) into two perfectly formed cakes, of convenient size for toilet use.

The price, compared to the quality and the size of the cakes, makes it the cheapest Soap for everybody for every want. TRY IT.

SOLD EVERYWHERE.

Until Procter & Gamble ran this advertisement for Ivory soap in 1882, it spent no money for advertising its products to the public. The company would eventually have one of the largest advertising budgets among U.S. businesses.

line of products, including Tide laundry detergent, Crest toothpaste, and Crisco shortening. With such widespread brand recognition and so many different products, it is hard to imagine that the company was started by two immigrants toiling over a backyard kettle.

Wizards of Wall Street

Dow Jones and
The Wall Street Journal

THE "DOW JONES AVERAGES" ARE SO widely quoted that even people who do not invest in the stock market understand that these figures can show how the United States economy is doing. Yet few people know who Dow Jones was, or is.

Actually, there was no such person as Dow Jones. Charles Dow and Edward Jones are the people whose combined last names have been immortalized, or forever connected, with the stock market indexes. Dow is the one who deserves most of the credit for creating the news service that helps financial analysts keep abreast of the stock market ups and downs.

Charles Henry Dow was born on a farm in Sterling, Connecticut, in 1851. His was a grim childhood. His two brothers died young, and his father died when

Charles was six. Little is known of Dow's life for the next 15 years. But it is said that when a group of his associates were discussing the various jobs that they had held over the years, Dow silently began writing on a sheet of paper. When he finished writing, he presented them with a list of more than 50 jobs at which he had worked.

Of all the occupations he had tried, journalism interested him the most. He was only 21 in 1872 when he was hired as a reporter for the *Springfield* (Massachusetts) *Daily Republican*. He was promoted to assistant editor before long. After three years in Springfield, he quit to take a job in Providence, Rhode Island. He worked as night editor for the *Providence Morning Star and Evening Press*, but he eventually applied for a job with the larger *Providence Journal*. When he was told that the paper had no more reporting assignments to hand out, Dow replied that he didn't need any assignments. He knew how to get news, he said, and all he wanted was a chance to prove it.

Dow received his chance and made the best of it. In 1879 the *Journal* sent him to report on mining activity in the West. The assignment to cover the gold and silver strike in Leadville, Colorado, gave Dow his first close look at high finance. There were only two rugged pioneers living in Leadville when precious metals were first discovered there in 1877. Within two years, more than 2,000 prospectors had arrived, and they were mining legendary amounts

Charles Dow

of silver. During his stay there, Dow spoke with many financial experts and wrote vivid stories about the high-stakes money games being played in the Rocky Mountain mines. When he returned to the East Coast, he gave up his job in Providence and followed the money people to New York City.

Although he was known for his quiet, reserved nature, Dow had little trouble getting a new job. He was hired to report on mining stocks. Before long, his ability to uncover news and report it accurately earned him the trust of those involved in the stock market. Dow eventually took a job with the Kiernan News Agency, which delivered news on handwritten sheets to brokerage firms and banks in New York's financial district. In 1882 he formed Dow, Jones & Company, a stock market news service, with Edward Jones. Jones, a college dropout, had worked with Dow at Providence and again at the Kiernan News Agency.

Edward Jones was a Worcester, Massachusetts, man, five years younger than Dow. He had taken a separate path to New York City after working with Dow in Providence, and he quickly earned a reputation as a top-notch financial journalist. He could understand even the most complicated financial reports and write about them in a clear, crisp style. Unlike the studious Dow, Jones was outgoing and good-humored. He became a favorite of the stockbrokers and bankers who gathered nightly at The Windsor Hotel. There Jones collected the valuable

Stocks are small parts of ownership in a company. Ownership is usually divided among many shareholders, or owners. Stocks are traded—bought or sold—in stock exchanges, or **stock markets**. The most famous stock exchange is on Wall Street in New York City.

Edward Jones

bits of information that made the Dow, Jones & Company reports so popular.

Dow and Jones were assisted in their news-gathering operation by another former Kiernan employee, Charles M. Bergstresser. Bergstresser later became a silent partner in the company.

Despite the high-finance world in which it was operating, Dow, Jones & Company was about as sophisticated as a lemonade stand. The company's office was in a small, dimly lit room behind a soda fountain. The day's news was copied longhand, and the sheets were delivered to various business customers by messengers. If they overheard any news during deliveries, it was included in the next edition. Over time the news sheets evolved into a more conventional newspaper. In 1889 Dow, Jones & Company introduced an improved version of their news reports, which they called *The Wall Street Journal.*

During his 22 years in the New York business world, Charles Dow became an expert at researching and analyzing the stock market. Dow also developed the index that made the company a household name: the Dow Jones averages. According to Dow, you cannot tell how strong the stock market is by looking at individual stocks. On any given day, some stock prices might be up, some down, and some stable, for a variety of reasons. But if you take a certain number of representative stocks and determine their average price, then you can detect more meaningful trends in the market. Each day, the news

A **silent partner** is a person who has given a company some money with the expectation of sharing the money the company makes, but who has no say in how the company is run.

The 1893 headquarters for Dow Jones & Company

In the late 1800s, news-papers were delivered around New York City by a driver using a horse and cart.

media report the four Dow Jones averages: industrial, transportation, utility, and composite.

In 1899 Edward Jones left Dow, Jones & Company to join a brokerage firm. Three years later, Charles Dow sold his company to Clarence W. Barron, owner of the Boston News Bureau and the Philadelphia News Bureau. Barron's descendants continued to be the majority shareholders of Dow Jones & Company, Inc. in the 1980s. Dow's former business was quite successful at the time of his death in 1902 at the age of 51. But little did he realize that within a few decades, his would be the most revered name in the history of the financial markets.

Sears catalog from 1896

A Sales Circus

Sears, Roebuck and Co.

Richard W. Sears

DURING THE LATTER PART OF THE 19TH century, a wide gap of suspicion had developed between farmers and merchants. Farmers were particularly upset with the high markup charged by retailers, whom they saw as lazy scoundrels cheating them out of a fair price.

Ironically, the man who won their confidence in this era of distrust was Richard Sears, a man with such a flair for outrageous claims about his merchandise that he has been compared to circus promoter P.T. Barnum.

At first glance, it is hard to imagine anyone trusting a businessman whose advertising sounded like it had been written by a carnival huckster. It is even more difficult to explain Sears's success in light of the accounting shambles he made of his company with his habit of drumming up orders for products he did not even have. Yet this rural telegraph agent with the circus flair for showmanship built his company from scratch into the largest mail-order business in the world. It has since expanded into a corporate giant of such influence that it bills itself as the store "where America shops."

Richard Sears was born in Stewartville, Minnesota, in 1863. His fondness for doing business in a grand way came from his father. A blacksmith and wagon maker by trade, the elder Sears amassed a savings of $50,000 and then invested it all in a risky

A retail establishment, or store, that sells its goods through the postal system is called a **mail-order business**.

Below: Richard Sears started his merchandising career from a train depot in North Redwood, Minnesota.

farm speculation scheme. When the deal fell through, the man lost every penny he had. Crushed by failure, he died within a few years, leaving Richard, 16 or 17 at the time, as the family's chief breadwinner.

Sears studied telegraphy and landed a job in St. Paul, Minnesota, with the Minneapolis and St. Louis Railway. For Sears, the job was only a base of operations. He talked his way into a position as station agent in North Redwood, Minnesota. The young man never seemed to miss a chance to add to his weekly salary of six dollars per week. During his spare time, he began selling whatever he could get his hands on. He dealt in coal, lumber, and other goods, which he was able to ship by railroad at a discounted price.

In the summer of 1886, he stumbled upon an opportunity that would change his life and the concept of mail-order merchandising. A Chicago jewelry manufacturer sent a shipment of pocket watches to a local jeweler, who claimed he had never ordered them. The jeweler refused to accept them, and while the mess was being sorted out, Sears offered to take them. Sears paid $12 each for the watches and telegraphed fellow agents down the line to see if they wanted in on the operation. He then sold the watches for $14 to other agents, who in turn sold them for $16 or more.

The sale went so smoothly that Sears decided to try it again. He ordered more watches and sold them just as easily as he had the first time. Six months

A **discount** price is usually lower than the normal or suggested price of an item or service.

after selling his first watch, Sears had built up a business that dwarfed his earnings as a station agent. Taking his $5,000 profit, he moved to Minneapolis in search of a larger market.

The R.W. Sears Watch Company opened for business in a rented office furnished with only a kitchen table and a chair. While continuing to sell through his contacts along the railway lines, Sears attracted other customers with national advertising in newspapers. The business was so successful that, within a year, he moved to an even larger market—Chicago.

Sears decided that he could make more money if he bought watch parts and assembled his own watches to sell. His advertisement for a watchmaker was answered by an Indiana man named Alvah Roebuck. Sears hired Roebuck on the spot. The combination worked well, with Roebuck providing the labor and the technical expertise and Sears taking care of sales.

Sears's gift for selling was so powerful that by 1889 he had made enough money to retire. Sears sold the company and moved to the Iowa countryside. He invested $60,000 from the sale of his company in farm mortgages. A leisurely retirement, however, did not satisfy the energetic 29-year-old for long. After a month, Sears was eager to get back into the sales business.

Unfortunately, when he sold his company, he had agreed to a non-compete clause that prevented him from using his last name in business for three years.

Alvah C. Roebuck

The buyer of a business frequently will make the seller sign a **non-compete clause** that keeps the seller from legally operating another business that could take customers away from the original business. Among other things, the clause can specify the types of businesses to be restricted and the length of time the restriction is effective.

A company is said to make a **profit** when the money it earns from sales amounts to more than the cost of producing or buying the goods or service.

Merchants can usually maintain their profits by buying and selling in large quantities. Generally, merchants who buy large amounts of goods from a manufacturer will receive a discount on the price for each item. The merchants can then pass those savings on to customers, who are more likely to buy from a store that offers a lower price. While the merchants may make a smaller amount of profit on each item, they make more money in the end because they have sold much more merchandise than they would have at the higher price.

Back in Minneapolis, Sears started a mail-order business that he called The Warren Company, after his middle name. Then he persuaded Alvah Roebuck to buy the company. Roebuck renamed it A.C. Roebuck Inc. He later turned over half interest in the company to Sears, and named Sears as president. The pair again moved the company to Chicago. When the three-year restriction had passed, the company was reorganized as Sears, Roebuck and Co.

Working 84-hour weeks, Sears set out to challenge Montgomery Ward, the undisputed leader in the mail-order business. He would eventually pass Montgomery Ward in annual sales. Because of his upbringing in the rural Midwest, Sears understood farmers' distrust of big city merchants. To ease their fears, he advertised a revolutionary "Send No Money" policy. Sears's customers did not have to pay until they had received their goods and had a chance to examine them. Further, his prices were lower than those charged by his competitors. He could make up this loss of profit by buying and selling in large quantities.

Sears spent a great deal of time putting together a catalog of all the goods that his company had to offer. Because he was located in Chicago, the railroad hub of the Midwest, he had access to a great number of products. By 1895 the catalog had grown to more than 500 pages. Every space was filled with writing, and every word was written by Richard Sears.

The salesman in Sears could not resist the urge

for creating incredible slogans. He once described a new typewriter as "perfection perfectly perfected, yet simplicity simply simplified." His thick catalogs were distributed free of charge, and he pumped as much effort into advertising as any businessperson of his time.

Not only was his advertising shamelessly flamboyant, it often skirted the truth. In 1895 he proclaimed his company one of the largest clothing dealers in the country, and he offered great deals on suits. The problem was that Sears did not have any suits in stock! For the action-oriented Sears, there was nothing wrong with getting all the orders first and then trying to fill them. Unfortunately, that made life miserable for his shipping department, which had to cope with a large number of incoming orders and lack of stock. In the chaos that followed, sizes, colors, and fabrics ordered by the customers were hopelessly mixed up.

After Sears's tactics caused repeated delays in properly filling orders, the company's reputation began to suffer. Alvah Roebuck could stand the pressure no longer and sold his interest in the company to Sears in 1895. Sears's shortcomings as a manager were eliminated with the arrival of a new partner in 1896: Julius Rosenwald. Rosenwald took over the business aspect of the company, while Sears continued to turn out catalogs and advertisements. Sears and Rosenwald built the company up from $1 million in sales in 1896 to $10 million by 1900.

A business with two or more owners, or partners, like the business Sears formed with Alvah Roebuck, and later operated with Julius Rosenwald, is called a **partnership**. A business owned by just one person is called a **sole proprietorship**. Large companies with many owners are called **corporations**. Although the corporation has become the major form of business in the U.S.—providing the most jobs and generating the most income —most businesses are still sole proprietorships.

Right: The first Sears retail store opened in Chicago, Illinois, in 1925. Until then Sears, Roebuck and Co. sold its goods only through the mail.

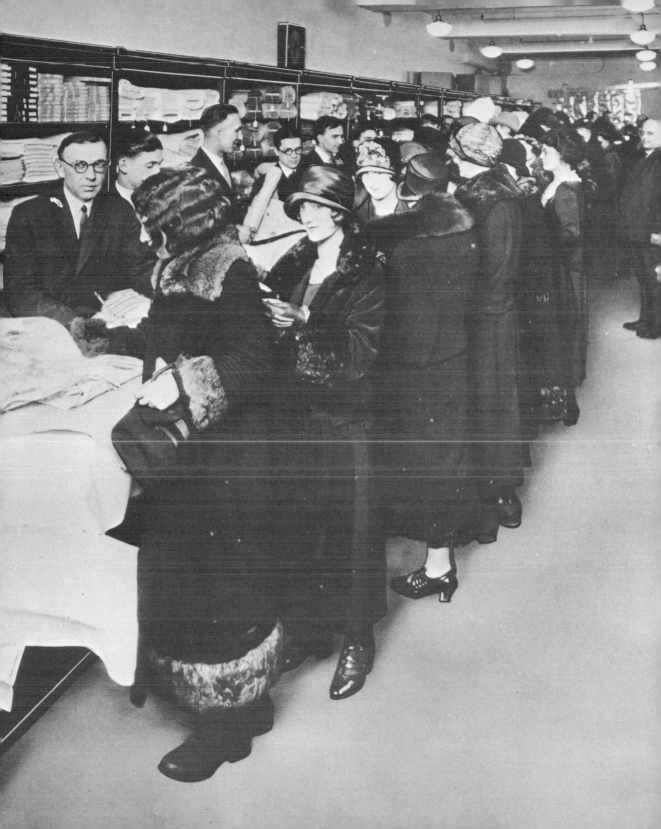

As Rosenwald's influence in the company grew, he began to challenge some of Sears's wilder ideas. In 1908 Sears proposed another ambitious promotional campaign. With the company trying to ride out a business depression, he wanted to increase promotional efforts by asking customers to supply the names and addresses of people they thought would be potential Sears customers. Rosenwald opposed the idea, saying the company needed to reduce expenses rather than increase expenses. After the company board of directors heeded Rosenwald's advice and refused to back the plan, Sears called it quits. He again retired, this time $40 million richer than he was when he sold his first watch.

In 1925 Sears, Roebuck and Co. turned away from its reliance on mail-order sales and began opening stores at which customers could walk in and shop for goods. Within four years, there were more than 320 Sears outlets in the United States. Although Richard Sears, who died in 1914 at the age of 50, did not live to see it, the corporation he had built grew into one of the 10 largest companies in the United States.

The Chocolate Factory
That Built a Town

Hershey

Milton S. Hershey

Henry Hershey BELIEVED IN DREAM-ing big. An avid reader, he was always exploring new ways to make money. Unfortunately, Hershey was more optimistic than successful. He was never able to earn enough money to fully support his wife, Fannie, or their son, Milton.

Later, when several of Milton's business ventures had failed, Fannie's family began to worry that he had become too much like his father and that he would always be in debt. But Milton proved them wrong. While the family would denounce the elder Hershey, Milton Hershey would make the most of his father's advice: "If you want to make money, you must do things in a large way."

Milton S. Hershey was born in 1857 on a farm near Derry Township, Pennsylvania. Milton's father was always certain that great success was just around the corner, and he pursued one improbable business plan after another. Nothing worked out.

With the various business ventures the elder Hershey tried, the family moved too often for Milton to get a solid education. By the time Milton was 14, he had less than a fourth-grade education. He dropped out of school to become an apprentice. Milton worked first as a printer's apprentice to the editor of a German-language newspaper in the nearby town of Lancaster. But he was clumsy and disliked the work. He was eventually fired for dropping a straw hat into the printing press.

His mother helped him to get his next job as an apprentice to a candy and ice cream maker in Lancaster. Milton found this job interesting enough to dream of going into business for himself. In 1876, after four years of learning the trade, he moved to Philadelphia to start his own candy store. The timing seemed to be perfect. Philadelphia was bustling with tourists celebrating the 100th anniversary of the Declaration of Independence. With money that he borrowed from his aunt Mattie, Milton rented a small building and began making penny candy.

The venture failed to produce the riches he had been expecting, although enough customers trickled in to keep the business going. After six years, however, Milton grew tired of the meager profits and sold it. Most of the money was used to pay off debts.

Milton then moved to Denver, where his father

A label used by Milton Hershey for his Philadelphia business

lived. He took a job with a candy-maker there. Before long, Milton and his father went into business together, making and selling candy in Chicago, Illinois. They went out of business shortly, however.

His father's new recipe for a cough drop took them to New York, where the two hoped to market cough drops along with their candy. This business came a bit closer to success than their other effort. But in 1886, Milton returned home penniless.

The travels had not been a complete loss, however. In Denver Milton had discovered that the secret to making good candy was fresh milk. Fresh milk was plentiful in the dairy region surrounding Lancaster. Milton experimented with candy until he came up with a delicious recipe for a milk-based caramel. Milton Hershey, the candy man, was back in business again. An importer from England happened to taste the caramels. The man was so impressed with the candy that he ordered a large quantity to send to England. Hershey was stunned when he received the order.

It was an opportunity that he could not bear to lose. Dashing off to the bank, Milton pleaded for a loan to buy more equipment. Because of Hershey's history of business failures, bank after bank refused to lend him the money. Finally, one banker agreed to lend the money. From then on, Hershey's Lancaster Caramel Company was a success. By 1894 Milton Hershey was one of Lancaster's most prominent citizens.

An importer is a person who brings goods for resale into a country from another country.

As his caramel business flourished, Hershey became interested in a new candy product. After receiving his first taste of a chocolate candy at the 1893 Columbian Exposition in Chicago, Hershey was so impressed that he purchased the chocolate-manufacturing equipment. When the exposition was over, the equipment was shipped to Lancaster.

At first Hershey's intention was simply to add a line of chocolate candy to his popular caramels. He used chocolate to coat some of the caramels. But the more he thought about it, the more Hershey was convinced that the public would eventually buy more chocolate than caramel.

He developed a mixture of sugar, liquid chocolate, milk, and cocoa beans that he was certain would be a success. In 1900 Milton Hershey sold his entire

After turning his caramel business into a huge success, Milton Hershey sold it. He then built a large chocolate factory in the heart of Pennsylvania's dairy industry.

The Hershey Industrial School, later renamed the Milton Hershey School, was founded to provide better opportunities for orphaned children.

Competition is one of the basic features of the U.S. business system. **Competition** means trying to get something that others are also trying to get. Producers compete for the best raw materials. Businesses compete with each other for the most customers. Companies compete to make the best-quality or lowest-priced product or service.

caramel business to his competitors for $1 million. In 1903 he began construction of a new factory in the middle of dairy farm country. The site he selected was his own birthplace of Derry Township.

Hershey built a town around his factory. He included a bank, school, churches, parks, golf courses, and a zoo. IIe also built affordable housing for workers who wished to live nearby. Because they were saddened by their inability to have children, Milton Hershey and his wife, Catherine, founded the Hershey Industrial School for orphaned boys in 1909. The school was later renamed the Milton

Hershey School and eventually began housing girls as well as boys. By 1989 it had the capacity to care for 1,250 boys and girls.

Many people thought Hershey was crazy for trying to start a big business in the middle of nowhere. But Hershey had guessed right. The public craved chocolate and bought as much as his huge plant could make. Sales of the five-cent HERSHEY'S milk chocolate bars grew rapidly. In 1911 sales passed the $5 million mark.

The company became so successful that soon no one could say the name "Hershey" without thinking of chocolate. It came to be identified with HERSHEY'S KISSES chocolates, REESE'S PIECES candy, and several different varieties of chocolate bars. Hershey Foods Corporation had sales of $1.7 billion in 1983.

Milton Hershey, once the penniless son of a penniless father, became fabulously wealthy. Yet, he never forgot the humble circumstances of his early days. When he died in 1945, Hershey willed the bulk of his fortune, including a controlling interest in the company, to the orphanage he had founded.

When a person owns stock in a business, he or she is said to have an interest in the business. In his will, Milton Hershey left a majority of the stocks, or a **controlling interest**, in the chocolate business to the Milton Hershey School. The school then had the most votes to cast in issues that came before stockholders at the Hershey Foods Corporation's annual stockholders' meeting.

The Golden Rule
Pays Off

J.C. Penney

James Cash Penney

A STORY TOLD ABOUT JAMES CASH Penney says that he kept his eye on the salt shaker whenever he sat down to dinner with someone. If his dinner partner salted the food before tasting it, Penney would not do business with him or her. If the diner was a prospective employee, Penney would not hire that person. Penney did not trust important decisions to people who jumped to conclusions before knowing the facts.

Whether the story is true or false, it captures J.C. Penney's personality. He was a man of strict principles, and he never wavered from his standards. Neither the most desperate circumstances nor the power of later wealth could budge him from following the Golden Rule upon which he built an empire: Treat others as you would have them treat you.

James Cash Penney was born on a farm in the country near Hamilton, Missouri, in 1875. The principles by which he lived were firmly impressed upon him by his father, a preacher. The elder Penney was an unpaid minister who supported his family of 12 children by farming a small plot of land. Money was always tight. When Jim was eight, his father told him that from then on the boy would be responsible for buying his own clothing. This came at a time when Jim needed a pair of shoes but did not have the money to buy them.

In order to raise the money, he worked odd jobs for his father. With the first $3.50 he earned, Jim spent one dollar for shoes. He thought about getting some clothes with the remaining money, but he figured he could make more money by buying and raising a young pig instead. With no money left over after the purchase to buy feed for the pig, Jim made agreements with several neighbors to take away table scraps for the pig to eat. In return, he cleaned their garbage pails. He fed the pig until it was ready for market, then sold it for a profit.

Figuring that if it worked once it ought to work again, Penney bought more pigs. After neighbors complained about the noise and smell from the yard full of pigs, Jim's father put a stop to the enterprise. He did not think it was fair for Jim to earn money while subjecting his neighbors to such inconveniences. Young Jim sold the pigs and looked for other ways to make money.

J.C. Penney as a young man

Penney, second from right, ran a meat market and bakery in Longmont, Colorado, before starting to sell dry goods again.

After graduating from high school in 1893 and working on the farm for a couple of months, Penney took a job as a clerk at a local dry-goods store, working for $2.27 a month. Later, health problems forced him to move out of the heat and humidity of Missouri to Denver, Colorado. There he found another clerking job at a department store. He left that store, though, when he discovered the owner was charging an unfair price for some merchandise. Penney then bought a butcher shop and bakery in Longmont, Colorado, with his $300 in savings.

It was not long before Penney's high principles were put to a stern test. His most important account was a large hotel in town. The chef at this hotel expected some under-the-table payments in exchange for doing business with Penney. All Penney had to do was slip the chef a bottle of bourbon each week, and the chef would see to it that the orders kept coming. In a weak moment, Penney gave in, but as soon as he did it he was disgusted with himself. After he refused to send any more bourbon, the orders stopped, and Penney went out of business.

He then went to work for T.M. Callahan and Guy Johnson, who owned dry-goods stores in the West. While working for a year under Johnson, Penney so impressed his bosses that they asked him in 1902 to join them in opening a new store. The price of a partnership was $2,000, far more than Penney had saved. Penney was able to borrow the money he needed. With his wife, Berta, and a baby son, he headed to Kemmerer, a southwestern Wyoming mining town of about a thousand people. Their living quarters were hardly deluxe—they lived in the attic above the new store.

Kemmerer was not a very promising place for Penney to start a retail business. Two other merchants had tried to operate clothing stores there, but they had failed. Penney's store was very small, and it was far from the center of shopping activity in town. In spite of the odds, J.C. Penney started building his empire from the Kemmerer store.

An **under-the-table payment**, sometimes called a kickback, is a secret payment of money or gifts that a person receives in return for doing business with another person or a company. By requesting a bottle of bourbon that he would keep for himself, the chef would receive something in return for spending his employer's money with Penney's butcher shop. Receiving under-the-table payments is considered to be an improper use of one's position and is sometimes illegal.

Most stores people shop at are **retail stores**, which buy goods from wholesalers and sell them to customers. A person who buys **wholesale** usually buys a large quantity of products directly from the manufacturer at a greatly reduced price. He or she can then sell the products to stores or businesses at a higher price.

Penney opened his first store in a small building in Kemmerer, Wyoming, in 1902. Within five years, Penney was on his way to establishing a chain of stores.

Penney later recalled that other merchants and bankers laughed at the name Golden Rule store. They could not believe that Penney's high-minded principles would survive in the cutthroat world of business. But Penney was determined to prove that a person could be both fair and successful in business.

He carefully studied the needs of the townspeople and made sure he bought good-quality merchandise. Unlike many merchants of the time, Penney marked the price on each item rather than trying to haggle the most he could get out of each customer. Some of his other innovations included the introduction of odd-amount prices (such as the now popular "$X.99$") and an emphasis on courteous, personal service to all customers. His skill at evaluating job applicants, combined with his careful training program, helped to make shopping in his store a far more pleasant experience than most people were used to in the small town.

By conducting **training programs**, a business can teach employees skills that they will use when working for the business. Each worker, regardless of how skilled she or he is for a job, generally needs to learn certain details about how a company does its business—how it greets customers, how it reports sales, and so on.

Merchandise in Penney's stores carried price tags so customers could tell how much each item would cost them.

From the beginning, Penney proved the cynics wrong. In his first day, he rang up more than $466 in sales, even though suspenders were priced at five cents, and petticoats sold for 29 cents. Merchandise continued to move briskly throughout the year. With growing evidence that he was on the right track, Penney began thinking about expanding into a small chain of Golden Rule stores. As he invested in another store the other partners owned, then opened yet another store with them, he thought more about the partnership plan. He was sure other capable store managers would appreciate the chance to own part of their own business just as he had in Kemmerer.

In 1907 when Johnson and Callahan sold Penney their interests in the three stores they owned with him, Penney was free to carry out his proposal as aggressively as he saw fit. He selected the hardest-working of his clerks and offered them partnerships under terms similar to those he had been given five years earlier by Johnson and Callahan. Within a few years, Golden Rule stores were opened in Utah and Idaho.

Leaving the day-to-day operations to his well-trained partners, Penney moved to Salt Lake City, Utah, in 1909 to coordinate buying and financing for the entire chain. Sixteen more Golden Rule stores opened in the next two years. Penney began to spend an increasing amount of time traveling to the East Coast to select merchandise for the stores.

By ignoring the major markets and concentrating

on running small stores in small towns, Penney had a chain of 36 stores by 1913. That same year, the business incorporated and changed its name to the J.C. Penney Company. The next year, Penney moved the company's offices to New York City to make buying and transporting goods easier.

J.C. Penney Company's first "big city" store opened in Salt Lake City in 1917. By then the company had grown to 175 stores. That same year, at the age of 42, Penney became chairman of the board and devoted his time to recruiting and training new employees.

The J.C. Penney Company continued to grow at a rapid rate. In 1927 the company marked its 25th anniversary and had 892 stores and more than $151 million in sales. At the time, Penney predicted that

Many people choose to **incorporate** their business, or form a corporation. Corporations have several advantages over businesses that are not incorporated. By filing for incorporation status with the government, business owners can limit their financial risk. For example, if the business fails, they will not lose any of their personal belongings, like cars or houses. They will lose the money they used to buy stock in the company, however.

A corporation can issue additional stock to raise large sums of money. A corporation can also deal with the retirement or death of an owner without undue disruption of business operations.

A modern-day
J.C. Penney store

In later years, Penney reduced his involvement in managing the chain of stores that bore his name. Yet he still dropped in at various J.C. Penney stores around the country to serve customers.

In general, an economic **depression** is a period when making, buying, and selling products and services slow down. It is a time marked by unemployment and business failures, and people do not have much money to live on. In the 1930s, the United States suffered through a period called the **Great Depression**, during which the U.S. economy was paralyzed.

the company would reach $1 billion in sales by its 50th anniversary. In 1951, 49 years after the first of Penney's stores opened, the company achieved that landmark.

Despite his poor background, J.C. Penney amassed a fortune of about $40 million by 1929. He then lost almost all of it in the Great Depression. But Penney jumped right back into his business. For many years, he traveled among the stores, personally waiting on customers with the courtesy and helpfulness that he insisted was a salesperson's duty.

His long life ended in 1971 at the age of 95. By then he had seen the chain of stores built on his principles grow into a familiar fixture in large and small towns throughout the country.

The Shepherd's Root Beer Stand

Marriott

T HE MARRIOTT CORPORATION GREW phenomenally because of three goals the founder, J. Willard Marriott, established for himself when he went into business. Marriott's goals were: first, to provide friendly service to his guests; second, to provide quality food at a fair price; and third, to work as hard as he could—day and night—to make a profit. The formula helped a poor shepherd build his root beer stand into an empire.

John Willard Marriott was born in a small settlement near Ogden, Utah, in 1900. At first glance it would appear that he came from an influential, well-to-do family. After all, the town where he lived was named Marriott. It was named after Bill's grandfather, who had traveled to the Salt Lake City, Utah, area with a large group of Mormons (members of

Left: J. Willard Marriott stood in the doorway of his first Hot Shoppe, which he opened in 1928.

the Church of Jesus Christ of Latter-day Saints) in 1851. Four years later, the family traveled several miles to the north and started its own settlement.

Bill's parents owned a sugar beet farm and also raised thousands of sheep. But even when the farm was mildly profitable, life was never easy for the Marriotts. The sheep grazed on a huge range, and they had to be watched carefully. Wild animals frequently tried to attack sheep on the range. At the age of eight, Bill was sent off into the hills to spend nights with the other shepherds, keeping watch over the animals. He braved harsh weather, rattlesnakes, and bears.

Marriott was given responsibility early. When Bill was 14, his father sent him by freight train with 3,000 sheep to sell them in San Francisco. The next year he took 1,000 head on a longer trip to Omaha, Nebraska.

Like all young male Mormons of the day, Bill Marriott was required to serve as a missionary when he turned 19. He traveled around the New England states, trying to convert people to the Mormon faith. By the time he returned to Utah two years later, the price for sheep had plunged from $14 a head to $3. His father had borrowed far too much money to keep the farm going and was heavily in debt.

Bill saw that his father would have to make payments to the bank for the rest of his life. He was determined that he would not suffer the same fate. A college education, he thought, would be his

Debt is an obligation to pay something, like a bill. Because he had borrowed so much money to continue operating the farm, Bill Marriott's father had many bills to pay for several years.

J. Willard Marriott

chance to get off the farm. To raise money for college and for the family, Bill and a friend sold woolen underwear for a textile mill. They worked all summer, traveling from logging camp to logging camp. At the end of the summer, they each had earned more than $3,000 in commissions. Bill enrolled at Weber State College in Ogden, Utah, for a two-year program. After he graduated from Weber, he went to the University of Utah in Salt Lake City for two years.

Between the missionary work that delayed his college education and taking off another year to work on the farm, Bill was nearly 26 years old when he graduated from the University of Utah. He worked at Weber State College for a year. But he soon decided to go into business for himself.

One of his more enjoyable discoveries in college was a delicious new root beer formulated by two men with the last names Allen and Wright. This new "A & W" root beer proved to be quite popular in Salt Lake City during the hot summer months. The owners of the A & W franchise appeared to be making a large sum of money from the business. Bill Marriott began to think about setting up his own stand, if he could find the right location.

He remembered that he had watched street vendors in Washington, D.C., when he was there after finishing his missionary work. In the hot, humid summer, they sold their soft drinks so quickly that they constantly had to leave to get more beverages to sell. An A & W root beer stand would certainly be successful there.

In the spring of 1927, Marriott traveled to Washington, D.C., with $1,500 he had saved and another $1,500 he had borrowed from a bank in Utah. He was engaged to marry his college sweetheart, Allie Sheets, when she graduated in June, so he had two months to establish a business before bringing her to Washington, D.C. He formed a partnership with Hugh Colton, who was also from Utah. Colton worked for the government during the day and attended law school in the evening. Bill would run the root beer

Location is an important part of launching a new business. Before opening new restaurants, Bill Marriott would scout for good locations. He would park his car near each location he was considering and count cars passing by in each direction at different times of the day—lunchtime, 5:00 to 8:00 in the evening, and 10:00 P.M. to midnight. By checking into the traffic near each possible location, Marriott could tell which places would have the greatest potential for drawing customers.

Allie Marriott

stand, and Hugh would contribute $3,000 and be part owner in the business.

They set up shop in part of a bakery in a residential area more than a mile from downtown. They installed a large, revolving, orange-colored root beer barrel on the counter near the display window to attract customers from the street. They also passed out coupons for free root beer on street corners.

Because it was an especially muggy summer, Marriott's stand was soon so busy that he, Allie, and Hugh Colton were able to open a second stand in Washington, D.C., that same summer. But as soon as the weather cooled in the early fall, root beer sales dropped off. Marriott tried to think of a way to make the business profitable during the winter. Rather than try to get people to buy root beer in cool weather, Marriott decided to change with the seasons and give the customers what they wanted. If cold drinks made them feel better in the summer, then it was logical that they would crave hot food in the winter. He decided to serve spicy Southern and Mexican foods like chili, hot tamales, barbecued beef sandwiches, and hot dogs. The only problem was that neither he nor Allie knew how to make the hot tamales and chili they wanted to offer.

Borrowing some recipes from a friendly chef at the Mexican Embassy in Washington, D.C., Marriott stormed into action. After running the root beer stand one day, he, Allie, and Hugh worked all night to convert the place into a cafe. By morning the huge root beer barrel had been torn down, the store-front repainted, and stoves installed. Marriott's Hot Shoppe, a family-style restaurant, was ready for business without losing a day.

Marriott often said that no one could get anywhere in business by working only 40 hours a week, and he lived what he preached. During those first years, he rose early to be ready for a 9:00 A.M. opening, and didn't finish cleanup until well after midnight. In between he would wait on customers while Allie cooked the food.

That work schedule paid off. The Hot Shoppes were so successful that Marriott was able to buy out Colton's share of the business in 1928. During the next five years, while the rest of the country suffered through the Great Depression, Bill Marriott made a million dollars. With five Washington, D.C., Hot Shoppes in operation by 1932, he was far beyond the struggling stage. But his relentless working hours had to be curtailed when he was diagnosed with Hodgkin's disease—cancer of the lymph glands—in 1934. Doctors told Marriott he had between six months and a year to live. After six months, however, the doctors could find no sign of the disease, and Marriott was back at work.

Marriott kept his eyes open for new opportunities to meet customer needs. One day a Hot Shoppe manager told Marriott that some of the restaurant's customers were taking their meals onto airplanes at nearby Hoover Field airport in Washington, D.C.

Right: Marriott's second Hot Shoppe, a drive-in, was a popular eating spot for people in Washington, D.C. Bill Marriott posed in front of the sign that featured the Hot Shoppes symbol of a "running boy."

Marriott began an airline catering business that loaded food onto airplanes before takeoff. Flight attendants then served the light meals during airplane trips.

Airlines did not serve refreshments then, but Marriott thought that airlines might want to provide their passengers with meals during flights. The very next day, he proposed to supply Eastern Air Transport with food for flights leaving Washington, D.C. He got the contract and created an airline catering business.

During World War II, Marriott discovered that many government and factory workers had no place to eat. He then opened cafeterias in a variety of places such as factories, hospitals, and colleges. The catering portion of the Marriott business eventually

A **contract** is a business arrangement in which one person or business agrees to supply another person or business with a certain amount of goods and services at a fixed price.

grew to serve more than 100 airlines and more than 2,000 cafeterias.

But it was not until 1957, almost 30 years after opening his root beer stand, that Marriott got into the business for which he is most famous—hotels. That year Marriott opened the Twin Bridges Marriott Motor Hotel in Washington, D.C. Within another 30 years, nearly 500 Marriott-operated hotels opened around the world. The usual Marriott emphasis on providing comfort eventually proved to be a valuable trait in the business. The attention given to minor details was one way of guaranteeing customer satisfaction.

There was a time when Bill Marriott could provide seats for only nine customers in his first A & W stand. That root beer stand, opened by a former shepherd, was the beginning of a corporation that would eventually operate throughout the United States and in 26 foreign countries.

David Packard adjusts Hewlett-Packard's first major product, an audio oscillator.

The Garage That Started Silicon Valley

Hewlett-Packard

DAVID PACKARD, CHAIRMAN OF THE board of the Hewlett-Packard Company, glared at his watch. He had set an important meeting for 8:00 A.M. sharp. It was nearing 8:30, and there were still empty chairs. After watching a few more latecomers slink into the room, Packard fumed, "The next person who walks in that door doesn't deserve to work at Hewlett-Packard." The tension instantly dissolved when Packard's partner, Bill Hewlett, showed up next. The idea that Hewlett didn't deserve to work for the company he helped start was laughable.

Even though it is a large business that competes in a cutthroat, high-technology field, Hewlett-Packard has a reputation as a company that treats its employees well. Perhaps that homey attitude comes from the longtime employees who remember that

Hewlett and Packard began their operations in a garage.

William Hewlett was born in Ann Arbor, Michigan, in 1913. When he was quite young, his family moved to Palo Alto, California. His father had accepted a position teaching medicine at Stanford University. After high school, Bill attended college at Stanford, where he met David Packard, a Pueblo, Colorado, native. Both received their degrees in 1934 and went their separate ways to pursue master's degrees in electrical engineering.

The two remained close friends, however. After a few years, they talked about going into business together. During the late 1930s, they began to spend more and more time tinkering with equipment in a garage behind the house that Packard was renting.

For a while, they had trouble thinking of something to invent. The first three inventions—an automatic urinal flusher, an automatic foul indicator for bowling alleys, and a shock machine to help people lose weight—were not practical and did not sell.

After those failures, they began to spend more time developing an audio oscillator, a device that would measure the intensity of recorded sound. At first Hewlett and Packard couldn't sell the oscillator. A friend, however, wondered aloud whether Hewlett and Packard's device could be used in preparing sound tracks for movies. He talked to a friend at Walt Disney Studios about the possibility.

The Disney engineer, as it turned out, was very

David Packard, left, and Bill Hewlett

Packard, sitting, and Hewlett manufactured their first products in Packard's garage. They moved to an office building shortly after filling an order for Walt Disney Studios.

The term **working capital** refers to the amount of money a person or company has available to run the business. Capital can be used to pay for materials and supplies needed to make products, as well as other costs involved in operating a company.

interested in the invention. Working in Packard's garage with a drill press, a few hand tools, and slightly more than $500 of working capital, Hewlett and Packard produced eight oscillators for Disney.

That was the break they needed. Production of their 200B oscillator (so named simply because the number sounded big) soon caused the business to outgrow the garage. Hewlett and Packard moved to a nearby building and hired their first employees. It was not until several years later, however, that the founders assigned other employees such tasks as sweeping floors, keeping the books, and taking inventory of their products. Until then they had done those chores themselves.

As the business demand for electronic measuring instruments grew, Hewlett-Packard, which became known as HP, expanded as well. With their innovative management techniques (they were one of the first companies to provide medical insurance and flexible hours for their employees), they were able to recruit and keep many of the most talented people in the business. Hewlett-Packard was a pioneer in the use of semiconductors, which most often are made of silicon. The company's growth attracted an entire new semiconductor and computer-chip industry that developed near HP's headquarters. It was an area that the media nicknamed "Silicon Valley."

By the early 1960s, Hewlett-Packard measuring systems were capable of producing information so fast that researchers couldn't keep up with it. This led the company to produce its first computer in 1966.

In 1968 the company developed the revolutionary HP 9100 calculator. Unlike previous models, this one was so small that it could be held in a hand. When Hewlett saw it, he congratulated the people who invented it, then challenged them to make one that would fit in his pocket. His request was taken

Keeping the books, or **bookkeeping**, refers to the process of recording business transactions, like money received and money paid out. By keeping such records, a company can tell if it is making money or losing money.

The products a manufacturer, company, or store has on its property are referred to as **inventory**. When taking inventory, people write down which items and how many of each are on the property.

A basic rule of business involves supply and demand. The number of products that are offered for sale at different prices at a certain time is called **supply**. **Demand** is the number of products that people are willing to buy at different prices at a certain time.

The HP-35, developed by Hewlett-Packard engineers in 1972, was the first scientific calculator small enough to fit in a person's hand.

so seriously that researchers even measured his pocket. The result was the HP-35, introduced in 1972. Along with paring down the size, Hewlett-Packard engineers had slashed the price from $4,900 for the HP 9100 to $395 for the HP-35. This invention is credited with making the slide rule obsolete.

Bill Hewlett and Dave Packard continued to work together until Hewlett retired in 1987. By then their original $500 investment had been transformed into a company with more than $7 billion in sales each year.

Apple II computers are used by students in class and at home.

The Seeds of
A New Industry

Apple Computer

Not long ago, computers were monstrous machines. They were so big in the 1940s that each one filled a large room. It would have been hard to guess that the bewildering fortress of switches and vacuum tubes would evolve into a computer that could fit on a person's lap. It would have been even more difficult to predict that some kindergarten children would be operating computers before they even knew how to read.

Until the 1970s, scientists and technicians were nearly the only people using computers. It took a couple of jeans-clad college dropouts to make a computer that could be used in classrooms and homes. Starting a small business in a garage, they sowed the seeds of a new computer industry.

One person responsible for developing personal

computers was an electronics wizard, Stephen Wozniak. By the time Wozniak reached his teenage years in the early 1960s, the invention of transistors, which replaced vacuum tubes and switches inside the computer, had decreased the size of the machines. Computers were more than just a hobby for Wozniak; they were a new world to be explored. He explored computer technology with such enthusiasm that, by the age of 13, he was designing computers. He won first place in a school science fair with a calculator that he assembled from his own design.

Dropping out of college during his junior year, Wozniak went to work for Hewlett-Packard. He proved to be a skillful designer of integrated circuits, devices that made electronic components smaller, yet more powerful than ever before.

Stephen Wozniak

Steve Jobs

For years Wozniak was fascinated by the idea of making a small computer that was faster than other computers and that could store more data. A new central processing unit— the "brain" of the computer— called a microprocessor, made such a small computer possible. In his free time, Wozniak had designed a small computer that was slightly larger than a typewriter. But while it had been a fun challenge for Wozniak, neither he nor Hewlett-Packard imagined there would be a widespread market for such a computer. But Wozniak's friend, Steven Jobs, saw a tremendous market among computer hobbyists.

Jobs and Wozniak met through a mutual friend when Wozniak was in high school and Jobs was a junior high school student. In high school, Jobs had

The **market** for computers or any other product or service means the potential buyers for that product.

been very enthusiastic about electronics, and he had worked at refining video games after high school, but he was not really interested in the inner workings of the machines.

Jobs's adoptive parents had moved from the San Francisco area to Los Altos, California, when Jobs was a young child. Jobs was a loner who never seemed to know where he fit in. He attended Reed College in Oregon for one semester before he dropped out. For a while he lived in a commune and tried various health diets. He became attracted to Eastern philosophy and, oddly, this is what drew him into the realm of video games. Jobs wanted to earn money for a trip to India, so he returned to California and talked his way into a job at Atari. There he was handicapped by his limited knowledge of electronics and his offensive personality. He worked at night because he couldn't get along with other employees.

In the summer of 1974, Jobs talked his supervisor into assigning him to a project in Germany. When he was done with his work there, Jobs traveled to India. But shortly after arriving, he contracted scabies and dysentery, and he quickly became disillusioned with the culture in India. Jobs continue to drift after returning to the U.S., working on and off at Atari. He continued his friendship with Wozniak, and was in a position to watch Wozniak develop his small computer. Jobs's enthusiasm for electronics was rekindled in 1976, when Wozniak showed him a computer board he had assembled.

While Wozniak took satisfaction in tinkering with the computer he had built for himself, Jobs had a vision of what Wozniak's microcomputer could do for the world. He imagined the work and time that these machines could save for ordinary people. Convinced that microcomputers could be used for word processing, education, business, and family finance, Jobs suggested that he and Wozniak form a company to manufacture and market computer kits.

The original Apple computer, the Apple I, was a crude-looking contraption, consisting of a computer board, that buyers could combine with a keyboard and monitor.

Despite his lack of technical abilities, Jobs brought to the partnership an intense, single-minded confidence. On April Fool's Day in 1976, Jobs and Wozniak formed the Apple Computer Company to sell computer boards, which could be used by hobbyists to create personal computers. They called it the Apple I. Jobs sold his van and Wozniak sold his scientific calculator to raise $1,350 for production of the boards. Working in the garage at the suburban house of Jobs's parents, they began making 50 boards that Jobs had managed to sell to a computer store. Jobs soon realized that they could earn more money by selling a complete computer.

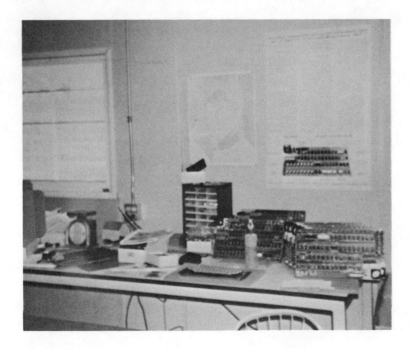

Wozniak and Jobs assembled circuit boards for the Apple I in a garage at the home of Jobs's parents.

This original Apple logo quickly gave way to a multi-colored apple with a bite-sized piece missing from the top right-hand corner.

Jobs left all the internal design work to Wozniak, but he made general suggestions about what the computer should be able to do and how it should look. Since Jobs envisioned selling to people who had not operated computers before, the new product had to be reasonably simple and "user friendly." It also needed to be light, trim, durable, and affordable.

In January, 1977, Jobs and Wozniak incorporated the company with a third partner, Mike Markkula. Markkula invested heavily in the business and helped the two founders plot market strategy. They moved out of the garage and into an office building. Three months later, their new computer, the Apple II, was ready. Jobs then started the sales promotion. With all the large, high-technology companies shying away from microcomputers, Jobs was free to develop the market. One of his plans was to capture the youth market by selling or donating Apple computers to school systems.

The Apple II computer caught on immediately and sales skyrocketed. Just as interesting as the sales reputation that Apple gained was the company's informal business atmosphere. Instead of wearing suits and ties, Apple executives often wore blue jeans to work. They occasionally attended corporate meetings barefoot. Many of the brightest computer experts, who felt stifled by the usual corporate procedures, sought employment at Apple.

The Apple computer was so successful that by

In 1977 Apple Computer moved into an office building in Cupertino, California, not far from the garage in which Jobs and Wozniak had started their business.

1981, 26-year-old Steve Jobs had already become a legend in the business world. By that time, Apple was earning hundreds of millions of dollars in sales.

Apple's reputation for manufacturing personal computers received a boost when the company introduced the Macintosh in January 1984. The Macintosh was revolutionary in the computer industry because it was the first computer that could be used by practically anyone, regardless of his or her computer knowledge. Complex command codes were replaced by a hand-held "mouse" that controlled an arrow on the screen. By pointing the arrow at words on top of the screen and pushing a button, the computer operator could display a host of commands and select one for the computer to perform.

The development of Apple Computer was interesting because it took three people with very different skills to get it off the ground. Stephen Wozniak had the technical expertise that he used to create a personal computer. Steven Jobs realized that Wozniak's invention was something that could be developed into a product that many people would buy. He had talent for marketing and finding ways to make the product appeal to customers. In addition to having money to start the business on a large scale, Mike Markkula had experience as a manager. He helped the company establish procedures for hiring employees, keeping books, and setting up dealerships, or retail stores, to sell the computers.

Apple continued to develop its products, introducing additional features with each new model.

Jobs, Apple president John Scully, and Wozniak (partially visible) introduced the Macintosh computer at a huge affair in 1984.

Both Jobs and Wozniak left Apple in the mid-1980s. Wozniak, in his 30s, eased into semiretirement, but Jobs lost a bitter power struggle over leadership of the company. The same aggressive traits that made him an excellent salesperson contributed to his downfall. In 1985 he was reassigned to a lower position in the company by the same people he had recruited to manage the company. He went on to pursue other business ventures in the computer field.

But by that time, less than 10 years after starting from scratch, the company he and Wozniak had

Although he helped to create Apple Computer, Steve Jobs did not own enough stock in the company to run it by himself. He fought with John Scully, the president of the company, for control of the company. Jobs wanted to run it his way. After this **power struggle**, Jobs was demoted, or given a less desirable position than he had held.

founded was worth billions of dollars. Two men working in a garage had launched the revolution that made computers an important tool of many small businesses and homes in the United States.

The Macintosh featured a new shape, a keyboard that could be moved away from the monitor, and a "mouse" that controlled an indicator on the screen.

For Further Reading...

Bryant, K.L., Jr. and Dethloff, H.C. *A History of American Business.* Prentice-Hall Inc., 1983.

Clary, D.C. *Great American Brands.* Fairchild Books, 1981.

Fucini, J.J. and Fucini, S. *Entrepreneurs: The Men and Women Behind Famous Brand Names.* G.K. Hall, 1985.

Livesay, H.C. *American Made: Men Who Shaped the American Economy.* Little, Brown & Company, 1980.

Moskowitz, M., Katz, M. and Levering, R., eds. *Everybody's Business.* Harper and Row, 1980.

Sobel, R. and Sicilia, D.B. *The Entrepreneurs: An American Adventure.* Houghton Mifflin Company, 1986.

Thompson, J. *The Very Rich Book.* William Morrow & Company, 1981.

Vare, E. and Ptacek, G. *Mothers of Invention: From the Bra to the Bomb: Forgotten Women and Their Unforgettable Ideas.* William Morrow & Company, 1988.

INDEX

Words in **boldface** are defined in the text.

ACKNOWLEDGEMENTS

The photos and illustrations in this book are reproduced through the courtesy of: pp. 1, 10, 12, 13, 14, 15, 16, 17, 18, Procter & Gamble; pp. 2, 58, 60, 61, 62, 63, Hewlett-Packard Company; p. 6, Kinney Shoe Corp.; p. 8 (top) Wal-Mart Stores, Inc.; p. 8 (bottom) Wang Laboratories, Inc.; pp. 19, 20, 21, 22, 23, Dow Jones & Company; pp. 24, 25, 26, 28, 31, 80, Sears, Roebuck and Co.; pp. 33, 34, 36, 37, Hershey Foods Corporation; pp. 39, 40, 41, 43, 44, 46, 47, J.C. Penney Company, Inc.; pp. 48, 51, 53, 55, 56, Marriott Corporation; pp. 64, 66, 67, 69, 70, 71, 72, 73, 74, 75, Apple Computer, Inc.

Cover illustration by Stephen Clement.

HERSHEY'S, HERSHEY'S KISSES, and REESE'S PIECES are trademarks of Hershey Foods Corporation and are used with permission.

A Sears, Roebuck and Co. store in El Paso, Texas, in 1934